# THIS BOOK BELONGS TO CERTIFIED GENIUS AUTHOR:

_____

# THE SCIENCE OF BEING A CHILDREN'S BOOK AUTHOR

## FUN & INTERACTIVE
### Book Creation Workbook

**EASY TO FOLLOW GUIDE FOR ALL AGES!**

**INCLUDES:**
- Book Creation Template
- 30-Day Self-Publishing Plan
- Coloring Pages
- Author & Self-Publishing Resources and much more!

AVA DISCOVERS HER INNER GENIUS
using
**S.T.E.M.**

Ava N. Simmons
Ava The S.T.E.M. Princess®

Thank you to the S.T.E.M. Leaders, Team Genius Squad Board members, key contributors all of the Geniuses around the world that support Team Genius Squad, I truly appreciate you for all of your support!

This Book Creation Workbook provides the basic fundamentals for authoring a children's picture book. It includes a book creation template developed and used by Ava N. Simmons to author and self-publish her first book. Since that time Ava has become an Amazon Best-Selling Author with an Amazon Best-Selling Book entitled, "Ava Finds Her Inner Genius Using S.T.E.M." The goal of this book is to encourage others to share their unique talents and stories with the world through self-publishing.

ISBN: 979-8-9860155-2-1
Book Type: Juvenile, Family

All inquiries regarding this book can be sent to the author at info@TeamGeniusSquad.com. For more information about the author or Team Genius Squad, please visit www.TeamGeniusSquad.com

# The Science of Being A Children's Book Author

## Lesson Plan

Topic: Writing, Book Creation

Learning Objectives:
After completing this workbook partcipants will learn the basics of how to become an author and self-publish a book.

Materials and Preparation:
• Book writing template workbook
• Writing and drawing utensils

Key Terms:
Author, Publisher, Self-Publishing, Illustrator, ISBN, Theme, Entrepreneur

Introduction (10 minutes)
• Gather the participants together in a comfortable area.
• Discuss exploring how to tell stories through writing.
• Each person shares a story title they could write about.
• Discuss the parts of a story; beginning, middle and end.
• Discuss the 5 steps to becoming a children's book author.
• Discuss how everyone is different and that our differences make us unique and special and this can be expressed through writing.

Activity: (35 minutes)
• Review the sample completed book author pages.
• Discuss story ideas.
• Write a Title, Character name, Beginning, Middle and End to a story.
• Draw pictures and write words on 3 pages to begin to share the story.
• Ask questions and share your great work with others.
• Take workbook home to complete the book creation template.

Learning Outcomes:
• Increased confidence in writing a book as the author.
• Increased confirmed exhibiting your creativity through drawing.
• Understand how to create a book using a template.
• Understand how to self-publish a book.

# THE FORMULA

# U + 5 = Children's Book Author

## U = YOU
## 5 = 5 STEPS

# LET'S GET STARTED!!

# The 5 Steps Overview

## STEP 1: Know that you have what it takes to be an Author & an Entrepreneur!

## STEP 2: Make Story Ideas Line For Your Book

Take your ideas and write a story title, story character, story setting, story beginning, story middle, and story end. Write the story information in your book template.

## STEP 3: Write Your Story For Your Book

Every day complete 4 pages, so you have a total of 28 pages to your story, including a front cover and back cover. Then draw pictures or use internet pic art, magazine, or newspaper cut outs, and write words to share your story on each page. Make sure you write the words clear or type your words and tape them to the page. When finished, recheck the book title to make sure it fits the story.

## STEP 4: Illustrate Your Story For Your Book

Corrections: Have someone review your story and check for spelling and grammar errors. Make the updates of any errors that are shared.

Illustrations: If you are the Illustrator, check to make sure the pictures match your story. Scan your story pages and save as a pdf file. If you would like to use another Illustrator, send your pdf file to an Illustrator. Request the Illustrator to finalize the book in 2 separate pdf files. One pdf will be the Front Cover and Back Cover as one pdf page size 17.391 x 11.25 inches. The other pdf file will be the inner pages that includes your story in size 8.625 x 11.25 inches. Please note: Your final book will be 8.5 x 11 inches, but you must add extra space around the edges of the page to ensure your text or pictures are not cut off during printing. We have made this easy for you by inserting a black border in the template pages to keep all work within the border. Make sure to request to review the Illustrators work before finalization.

## STEP 5: Publish Your Story for Your Book

Upload your story pdf files to a global publishing website, like Amazon KDP. Set up a free account and follow the step-by-step instructions to upload your pdf files. Retrieve an ISBN (International Book Identifier Number) from Amazon KDP for free.

Wait 72 hours for your book to be published on Amazon and while you are waiting, let your family and friends know that you are now a self-published author, and they can purchase your book on Amazon soon!

# The 5 Steps Quick Review

**1**

Know You Are An Author

Believe In Yourself

Be Confident

Know You Are A Genius

**2**

Make Story Ideas

Story Title

Story Character & Setting

Story Beginning Middle End

**3**

Write Your Story

Draw Pictures and Write Words

Check and Make Corrections

Save to a PDF file

**4**

Illustrate Your Story

Register On Fiverr

Find An Illustrator & send your pdf file

Review and Accept Final Illustration

**5**

Publish Your Story

Signup for Free Amazon KDP Account

Upload Your PDF File To Amazon KDP

Share With Others To Purchase Your Book

# Develop Your Story Line For Your Book

## Author
Write Your Name Here

_____

## Story Title
Write a title about the story you will write

_____

## Story Character and Setting
Write the name of the main character and setting of your story

_____

## Story Beginning (8 pages)
Detailed information of the character or setting, the topic, or the problem

_____

_____

_____

## Story Middle (9 pages)
More information about the beginning or when things begin to change

_____

_____

_____

## Story End (8 pages)
Information about how the story closes or the problem is solved

_____

_____

_____

Title: _____

**Add a picture (optional)**

Author: _____          Illustrator: _____

# Book Information Page

Thank you to _____

_____

_____

_____

_____ .

Text and Art Copyright ©2022 _____. All Rights Reserved.

This book was authored, including original art, and page scenes by_____

ISBN:_____
Book Type: Juvenile, Family

All inquiries regarding this book can be sent to the author at _____. For more information about the author please visit _____.

# Story Beginning

Write 1-2 sentences for each page of your story beginning.  Then write the sentences in the following pages with your drawing. See a completed example at the end of the workbook.

**Page 1** _____

_____

_____

**Page 2** _____

_____

_____

**Page 3** _____

_____

_____

**Page 4** _____

_____

_____

**Page 5** _____

_____

_____

**Page 6** _____

_____

**Page 7** _____

_____

_____

**Page 8** _____

_____

_____

# Example Of Making An Illustrated Story Book Page

## Book Page Process

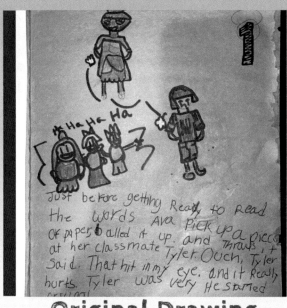

**Original Drawing**

**Clip Art E-version Drawing**

## SEND 1 or 2 TO ILLUSTRATOR

⬇️ Outcome From Illustrator ⬇️

Instead of reading to the class, Ava balls up a piece of paper and throws it at her classmate Tyler. "Ouch, that hit me in my eye and it hurts!", Tyler yells. Tyler then begins to cry and everyone starts laughing. Ava feels bad inside but now she doesn't have to read out loud and her classmates won't tease her; she is so relieved.

# How To Use The Book Template

Draw pictures in this area or use clip art to match
the story information you write.

Remember to keep your sentences and pictures within the dark
black border.

Write the 1-2 sentences on these lines to match the pictures.

Write your sentences in pencil so you can easily make corrections.

# Story Beginning Page 1

# Story Middle

Write 1-2 sentences for each page of your your story middle. Then write the sentence in the following pages.

**Page 1** _____

_____

_____

**Page 2** _____

_____

_____

**Page 3** _____

_____

_____

**Page 4** _____

_____

_____

**Page 5** _____

_____

_____

**Page 6** _____

_____

_____

**Page 7** _____

_____

_____

**Page 8** _____

_____

_____

**Page 9** _____

_____17

Story Middle Page 5

# Story End

Write 1-2 sentences for each page of your story end.
Then write the sentence in the following pages.

**Page 1** _____

_____

_____

**Page 2** _____

_____

_____

**Page 3** _____

_____

_____

**Page 4** _____

_____

_____

**Page 5** _____

_____

_____

**Page 6** _____

_____

**Page 7** _____

_____

_____

**Page 8** _____

_____

_____

# Story End Page 1

# Story End Page 2

# Story End Page 4

# Story End Page 6

# Back Cover
## (Add information about the Author Here)

(Add photo of Author Here, optional)

_____

_____

_____

_____

_____

_____

*ISBN Code will go here so
do not write in this area*

# Next Steps

1. Once all Story Book pages have been completed, have someone check your final story book pages for corrections and then make corrections as needed.

2. Cut or tear your Front Cover Page, Back Cover Page, Information Page, Story Beginning Book Pages, Story Middle Book Pages, and Story End Book Pages out of the workbook and scan them into an electronic pdf file.

3. With an adult sign-up for a Fiverr account at http://www.fiverr.com/s2/7fb9740fb9 (provides 10% discount) and find an Illustrator by inserting "Illustrator For Children's Books" in the search bar. When illustrator options show in a list, review and select 3 illustrators with 5 stars, Fiverr Pro status or Top Rated Seller status. Review their work to make sure it looks like something you may like. Then click their chat box circle and send the following request to the Illustrator(s) to check if they can meet your needs:

*Dear Illustrator,*

*I would like to request illustration of the attached 28 pages. Would you be able to provide:*
*-2 seperate high resolution pdf files prepared for an 8.5 x 11 inch paperback Amazon KDP publishing upload. One with the front and back cover and the second with the inner pages.*
    *-One pdf file: The illustrated inner page size 8.625 x 11.25 inches. This includes the bleed per Amazon KDP requirements*
    *-Second pdf file: The illustrated back page (on the left) and cover page (on the right) combined with a total size of 17.391 x 11.25 inches as one pdf page.*
    *-The source files for all illustrations.*
    *-An illustration with CMYK color.*
    *-Type the text on the page.*

*Please let me know:*
*-The cost per page and cost for all pages.*
*-How long it will take to complete the entire book illustration.*
*-How many revisions are included.*

4. With an adult sign-up for a free Amazon KDP account at Kdp.amazon.com so you can upload your pdf files once you receive the final illustration from the illustrator. Amazon KDP is free to publish your book. When you sell a book on Amazon KDP you will be sent a portion of each book sale.

5. Upload your 2 pdf files to your Amazon KDP account. The uploading process is very easy but their are VERY IMPORTANT STEPS for the PAPER BACK CONTENT tab that are critical to this process. On the PAPER BACK CONTENT tab you must ensure these 4 items are selected, 1. Publish Without ISBN, 2. Premium Color Interior with white paper, 3. Matte, and 4. Upload a cover you already have. Also ensure to click the "Launch Previewer" button to review your actual printed book and approve it. Amazon will require 72 hours to publish your book to their website.

6. Contact your family and friends and let them know you are an author and have self-published a book that will be available on Amazon.

7. Keep your original Story Book pages in a safe place to confirm the completion of your book.

# YOU DID IT!

# YOU ARE AN AUTHOR & AN ENTREPRENEUR!

# HELPFUL RESOURCES

**Free Self-Publishing Websites:**
* Kdp.amazon.com
* LuLu.com
* Bookbaby.com

**Freelance Children's Book Illustrators:**
* http://www.fiverr.com/s2/7fb9740fb9 (provides 10% discount)

**Free Clip Art Websites:**
* Freepik.com
* Vecteezy.com

**Keyword Definitions:**

**Story / Theme**
Details on real or not real characters and events.

**Author**
A writer of a book, article, or report.

**Publisher**
A person or company that prepares books for sale for an author.

**Self-Publishing**
An author that prepares their own books for sale.

**Illustrator**
A person who draws or creates pictures.

**ISBN (international standard book number)**
A ten-digit number assigned to every book for tracking before publishing.

**PDF (Portable Document Format) File**
An Adobe eletronic file format that provides text and images in a steady state with limited editing.

**Entrepreneur**
A person who owns and runs their own business or businesses.

# 30 DAY
# Self-Publishing Plan

## DAY 1
Know You Are A Author

Know that you are a GENIUS!

## DAY 2
Make Story Ideas

Write Title, Character, Beginning, Middle, End

## DAY 3
Write Your Story

Write 4 Pages

## DAY 4
**Activity Break**

Register For Fiverr Account at http://www.fiverr.com/s2/7fb9740fb9 to identify an Illustrator

## DAY 5
Write Your Story

Write 4 Pages

## DAY 6
Write Your Story

Write 4 Pages

## DAY 7
**Activity Break**

Search for 3 Illustrators on Fiverr and inquire about their services

## DAY 8
Write Your Story

Write 4 Pages

## DAY 9
**Activity Break**

Pick the illustrator you like from your 3 inquiries

## DAY 10
Write Your Story

Write 4 Pages

## DAY 11
Write Your Story

Write 4 Pages

## DAY 12
**Activity Break**

Contact family and friends to find 1 reviewer for your book

## DAY 13
Write Your Story

Write last 4 Pages

## DAY 14
**Activity Break**

Submit book for family/friend review

## DAY 15
**Activity Break**

Make review corrections and save as a pdf file

## DAY 16
Illustrate Your Story

Submit the pdf file to Illustrator

## DAY 17
**Activity Break**

Sign up for free Amazon KDP account at KDP.amazon.com

## DAY 18
**Activity Break**

Review Amazon KDP online instruction manual and think of a price for your book

## DAY 19
**Activity Break**

Notify family/ friends that you are now an Author and that they can buy your book on Amazon soon.

## DAY 20
**Activity Break**

Notify family/ friends that you are now an Author and that they can buy your book on Amazon soon.

## DAY 21
Illustrate Your Story

Review/Approve illustrations

## DAY 22

DAY OFF

## DAY 23
Illustrate Your Story

Review/Approve illustrations

## DAY 24
DAY OFF

## DAY 25
Illustrate Your Story

Receive final illustrations via 2 pdfs

## DAY 26
Publish Your Story

Upload 2 pdfs to Amazon KDP

## DAY 27
**Activity Break**

Notify family/ friends that you are now an Author and that they can buy your book on Amazon soon.

## DAY 28
**Activity Break**

Notify family/ friends that you are now an Author and that they can buy your book on Amazon soon.

## DAY 29
**Activity Break**

Send Amazon book purchase link to family/friends to buy your book

## DAY 30

**YOU ARE A SELF-PUBLISHED AUTHOR!**

# COLORING PAGES

43

# EXAMPLE OF COMPLETED BOOK PAGES

# Example of Completed Story Sheet

## Story Beginning

Write the words for each page of your story beginning. Then write the sentence in the following pages.

**Page 1**    Ryan is a Genius that loves school.

**Page 2**    When Ryan wakes up in the morning Ryan is excited because Ryan knows it's time for school.

**Page 3**    Ryan gets dressed and ready for school and picks out the best clothes.

**Page 4**    Breakfast is important to Ryan so it must be healthy.

**Page 5**    Ryan packs a good lunch for school with fruits and vegetables.

**Page 6**    Before leaving for school Ryan hugs mom and dad.

**Page 7**    The school bus has arrived and it's time to head to school.

**Page 8**    The ride on the school bus is fun and exciting for Ryan.

# Example of A Completed Book Page for
## Story Beginning Page 1

Ryan is a Genius that loves school.

Ryan is a Genius that loves school.

Thank you for taking the time to start your author journey with me. You are now a self-published author, entrepreneur, and member of Team Genius Squad!

Remember that you have purpose and unique talents; so, when challenges come your way focus on those great things within you. I found my inner Genius by focusing on my strengths and not letting my challenges shape my future; I want to encourage you to do the same.

I believe in you and can't wait for you to make your unique mark on the world with your new book!

Your Fellow Genius,

*Ava N Simmons*

**Ava N. Simmons**
**CEO, Team Genius Squad**

# MORE INFORMATION ABOUT THE AUTHOR'S SELF-PUBLISHED BOOK

## AVA FINDS HER INNER GENIUS USING S.T.E.M.
### (Science, Technology, Engineering, and Math)

**Author: AVA N. SIMMONS**
**Author Location:** Raleigh/Durham, North Carolina
**Subject:** S.T.E.M., Learning Challenges, Bullying

**Publish Date:** 8 April 2022
**Publisher:** Self-Published
**Trim:** 8.5 x 11 inches
**Page Count:** 42

**Format:** Paperback
**ISBN:** 979-8-986-01551-4
**Price:** $12.99

**Format:** Hardcover
**ISBN:** 978-0-578-78737-4
**Price:** $15.99

**Available from:** Author Website, Amazon

| HARDCOVER & PAPERBACK Author Website | PAPERBACK & KINDLE AMAZON |
|---|---|
| QR | QR |
| **Link:** https://shop.TeamGeniusSquad.com/collections/accessories | **Link:** https://www.amazon.com/p/B09XGVDZCJ |

**Sales, PR, and Marketing Contact**
Tita Simmons, Team Genius Squad Publications
**Tel:** 802-277-0332
**Email:** simmonstita@TeamGeniusSquad.com

**Media Coverage & Community Outreach**
- Forbes, AfroTech, Spectrum News
- Community S.T.E.M. Lab Truck Project Build

### Scan QR Code or Use The Links Below:

| Media Coverage Video & Articles | S.T.E.M. Activities in the Community Video | Community S.T.E.M. Lab Truck Build Video |
|---|---|---|
| QR | QR | QR |
| **Link:** https://www.teamgeniussquad.com/in-the-media.html | **Link:** https://youtu.be/J72dAPO00Jg | **Link:** https://youtu.be/HfxiFKxJL24 |

## About AVA FINDS HER INNER GENIUS USING S.T.E.M.

Have you ever or have you known someone who has been teased for not fitting within learning norms? Ava does, she was teased in school for not being able to read like her classmates. It significantly impacted her self-confidence and behavior. After several Principal office visits for not following classroom instructions Ava's parents intervened and confirmed that it's not just disobedience but rather an underlying issue. Once identified Ava turns to S.T.E.M. activities as a tool to help her overcome her learning and social challenges. This true story shares the learning journey and rise to stardom of 9-year-old Ava, also known as Ava The S.T.E.M. Princess®.

## Target Audience
- Children Ages 5-11 years old, grades K-5
- Children who learn differently (e.g. learning disorders, limitations)
- Children who experienced teasing, bullying, or social challenges
- Early readers and parents can read together
- S.T.E.M. Teachers and Enthusiasts

## Marketing
- National Book Chain Campaign
- Online & Print Review Campaign
- Social Media Campaign and Free Giveaways
- Media Interviews & S.T.E.M. Community Event Campaigns

## About Author AVA N. SIMMONS

Ava N. Simmons also known as Ava The S.T.E.M. Princess®, is a 9-year-old, S.T.E.M. Ambassador, Entrepreneur, Author, and Creator of the Team Genius Squad educational brand. Born and raised in Raleigh/Durham, North Carolina, Ava conducts educational S.T.E.M. experiments virtually and in the community via her Mobile S.T.E.M. Laboratory. She also designs S.T.E.M.-inspired products (e.g., lab coats, experiment kits). Ava is a Amazon Best Selling Author and has been featured in Forbes, AfroTech, and on Spectrum News. Team Genius Squad's mission is to share S.T.E.M.'s positive impact on critical thinking, reading, and math literacy. Additionally, to encourage others to believe in themselves no matter their challenges, identify their inner Genius, and never let their challenges define their future.

## Readings and Speaking Events
Ava is available for library readings, bookstore signings, classroom & community S.T.E.M. presentations. She is also, available for non-profit events.

## Visit Our Website
www.TeamGeniusSquad.com
**Follow Us on Social Media**
Scan QR Codes below or follow
@AvaTheSTEMPrincess on all platforms

| Website | Linkedin | Youtube | Instagram | Facebook |

# TEAM GENIUS SQUAD POSITIVE REMINDERS

I AM CAPABLE, CONFIDENT & STRONG!

I EMBRACE EVERY CHALLENGE!

I HAVE WHAT IT TAKES!

I NEVER GIVE UP!!

I AM TALENTED!

I BELIEVE IN ME!

I AM ENOUGH!

I AM UNIQUE!

I AM A GENIUS!

I AM AN AUTHOR!

I AM AN ENTREPRENEUR!

# STAY CONNECTED WITH TEAM GENIUS SQUAD

## Websites

Website: www.TeamGeniusSquad.com
Store: www.Shop.TeamGeniusSquad.com

## The Team Genius Squad APP

http://TeamGeniusSquadConnect.com/

## Social Media

♦ Instagram: @AvaTheSTEMPrincess
♦ Facebook: @AvaTheSTEMPrincess
♦ Twitter: @AvaTheSTEMPrin1
♦ LinkedIn: @AvaTheSTEMPrincess
♦ LinkedIn: @TeamGeniusSquad
♦ YouTube: https://YouTube.com/c/AvaTheSTEMPrincess

## Mailing Address

Team Genius Squad
8311 Brier Creek Parkway, Suite 105-260
Raleigh, North Carolina, 27703  USA
Tel: 802-277-0332
Email: info@TeamGeniusSquad.com

69195792R00035